CW00548342

save

me

an

orange

hayley grace

copyright © 2024 hayley grace
save me an orange
ISBN: 9798990047709

cover design by hayley grace, featuring artwork by JJ
Design House, © 2024 used under license. courtesy of MHS
Licensing.

all right reserved. no part of this book may be reproduced,
distributed, or transmitted by any means without the prior
written permission of the author.

save me an orange

to anyone who thought
the world would end
at 16

save me an orange

contents

introduction

7:00 am my mom woke me up for
elementary school
i told her i didn't feel good so i could stay in bed a
little longer

she handed me a slice of an orange and told me it
would make me feel better
i took the little piece of fruit and swallowed it
mom was right
she usually tends to be

3:00 pm i got off the bus crying because the boys
bullied me in middle school
i sat at the table with my mom
she handed me a slice of an orange
i ate it and swallowed my tears

11:45pm i came stumbling home drunk after some
stupid boy shattered my heart into pieces

my mom laid with me in my bed and consoled me
she asked if we could split an orange
i told her an orange couldn't fix this
she frowned and walked away

i would continue to lay in my bed just about
all summer
school started
but i didn't get out of my bed

the days seemed to be painfully long
and i became tired
a year went by
and all i wanted to do was sleep
mom was worried now

7:00am i sat at the breakfast table for what i
thought would be my last time.
but then my sister turned to me and asked me if i
could split her orange with her
with tearfilled eyes i agreed

she followed up by asking me if i could drive her
to school the next day
she said if i did she would buy me starbucks
all i could think about was tomorrow
there had to be a tomorrow.

maybe if i stayed a little longer
and shared an orange with a person i loved
or took a hot shower
or read one more page of my book
then the world would feel like something i
could hold

so i went to school the next day
with an orange in my backpack
and split it with my sister on the way home

———

1

the roots

the boys bullied me at school
i'd get off the bus in tears
making fun of the things
i could not change

i'd run home to my father
they tease you because they like you
he'd reply

-i guess my father was the bully too

_____

sometimes fathers teach their daughters
to confuse abuse with love

it may have worked on your mother
do not let it work on you

―――

whenever i see little girls with their fathers
part of me prays that he is a good man
because there is a difference
between being a good father
and being a good man

that thought keeps me up at night
i'm not sure if my father is a good man

i'm sure you have heard that saying
the one about women being attracted to men who
embody similar qualities as their father

every time i have a relationship with a guy i notice
a pattern
i'm constantly begging for them to stay
or begging for their approval
just like i've done my whole life with my father

maybe if i do this he will love me more
or maybe if i act this way he will see me for what
i'm worth
if i stand up straight and do what i'm told
maybe the next guy will think i'm enough

most guys look at me the way my father used to
look at my mother
i pretend not to notice it
until they call me and tell me they made a mistake

or they were drunk and they didn't mean to
kiss her

i'll lock myself in the bathroom sobbing on the
other end of the phone as i stare into the mirror

i stare at my mother
but she's blonde with blue eyes
and i'm brunette with brown eyes

i'm not my mother
i can't be my mother

as i grew up i think my dad stopped looking at me
as his child
but as my mother's daughter

my reflection stares back at me through the
bathroom mirror

i begin to see the resemblance
the one between my mother and i

fuck.
i look just like my mother

_____

i think i was forced to grow up *fast*
because my parents could not

i was only 9

———

my sister thinks i hate her
i think she confuses hatred
with jealousy

i've never hated my sister
i envy her

i'm jealous of her childhood
of the secrets that were kept from her
because she was *too young*

i may have been a little older
but i was a child
i deserved that childhood too

but if one of us had to grow up fast
i'm glad it was me
i couldn't live another day
if i had to watch her go through
the things that i did

so if the price of letting her live
and be a kid
is having her think
that i *hate* her

i guess that's the price i'll have to pay

maybe one day she'll see it how i do

_____

the boy you meet when you're 16
is supposed to be your first heartbreak

not your father

can you put my pieces back together

———

i stopped getting excited for birthdays
and holidays
and nights out with friends
it seemed as though the only thing that could
excite me
was watching the numbers drop from the scale

a medium iced coffee no sugar and oat milk please
i'd order at the local coffee shop
with lifeless eyes and the sound of my stomach
crying out of hunger

 i don't even like coffee

you're not hungry you're just bored
my father used to tell me
as i got off the bus asking for an afterschool snack

so i started chewing gum

i find myself to be a competitive person
but this was different
this time
it was me against myself
i was never gonna win

the mirror was my worst enemy
every time i stood in front of it
my reflection looked back at me

fingers pinching skin i wanted to lose
and hair falling out of my head

but if i put all the food i ate in a day
on a plate
in front of a fourth grader

would she still be hungry
would i let her starve?
would she tell me her stomach is still growling?

i can't let her stay hungry
she needs to eat
that little girl still lives inside of me
i needed to do this for her

i went to my mother
and she looked at me and said

what would you be if no one could see your body
who would you be if there was
no scale
no mirror

she looked at me with the eyes of a mother
who once saw herself in her daughter
and said
your appearance will always be
the least interesting thing about you

so have a slice of cake on your birthday
and have a soda with your friends
and while you're at it
share an orange with your sister
she's only in 4th grade
you don't want her to starve now
do you?

_____

the little girl in me
still craves the love
my father could not give

_____

i read a quote that said
when you're born in a burning house, you think
the whole world is on fire. but it's not.

i never really thought my house was burning
i mean i always had 2
2 houses
2 beds
2 front doors
2 birthdays

i mean as a kid i thought i had it all
i didn't see anything wrong with this way of life
because it was all i ever knew
my parents didn't love each other
but they loved me
they made sure to tell me that often

my mom was born in a burning house
we talk about it sometimes
she couldn't escape the fire
so that's where we live now
you can still smell the smoke
in the kitchen

i idolize my dad for putting out the fire
but his house still has water damage
we don't really talk about what caused the fire
he usually just shuts me down
so i stopped asking

i started dating boys
it never works out
they remind me of my dad

i wonder when he will tell me what caused the fire

i never really thought i was born in a
burning house
but whenever i meet someone new
and we talk about their family
my first question always is
are your parents still happily married?

———

"hey mom can you pick me up from school i have
a headache"
"mom can you make pancakes for breakfast …
the ones with the cinnamon"
"mom do you think i could have five dollars for
ice cream"
"hey mom i know it's late i just forgot how many
pills i'm supposed to take"
"should i take them with food"
"mom why did you and dad get divorced"
"is depression hereditary mom"
"mom i'm sorry i haven't called in a while i've
just been busy"
"mom i really don't want to talk to you but i need
you to tell me it's gonna be okay"
"mom i'm sorry i stopped coming around"
"mom why did you have to give me your nose"
"can you fix it"
"why can't anyone fix me mom"
"am i always gonna be just as broken as you"
"mom i wanna be a little girl again"
"mom i miss when you felt like my mom"
"i do want to be around you but it's so hard"
"i'm trying to let you back in"
"but mom i don't remember when i stopped"
"mom why does it still hurt"
"does it still hurt you"
"do the people in your head still fight the way
they do in mine"

"mom i can't come over"
"i'm sorry mom"

your story can't be mine too

———

my mother gets angry with me

not the same angry my father got with her

she doesn't scream or raise her voice
she doesn't use the strength of her hands
yet somehow her words hurt more than fists
ever could

sometimes she makes up scenarios in her head
writing her own fictional novel
casting me as the antagonist

for as long as i have my father's eyes
i think i'll always be the villain

she'll paint herself the hero
claiming she tried to save me from my
father's rage
but she was just a little too late

she'll write that he brainwashed me
and that i'm just an echo of him
repeating back everything he says

but it's not true you know
these fictional novels are delusions she will
feed herself
so she can stop being afraid of the fact

that when she looks at me
she sees all the things she could've been.

and i don't know what's scarier

to know that the woman in which i built a home
inside of sees me as a villain?

or that when i look at her i realize

she. is. all. i. might. be.

———

my parents told me i didn't know what love
really was
but how would they know
my mother thought she picked the finest orange
but my father turned rotten
spoiled fruit is what she called him

for the first time in a while
i believed i was beautiful
because he told me i was beautiful
i was just beginning to see life in color
and isn't that what love is about
finding someone who guides you through
the darkness
and shows you the light

give me the rose colored glasses

––––

i want someone to look at me
and tell me the things they don't like
and i know that's a strange thing to ask
but could i just put my clothes back on for
a second
it'll only take a second
i'm sure you would be able to think of something
something
anything
one thing you don't like
because
i could tell you a million things
like how i've never liked my nose
and how i have terrible posture
and if you look at me for a second
just a second
maybe you can see that my eyebrows are uneven
or if i just put my clothes back on you would
notice how i crack my knuckles when i'm nervous
maybe you'll see how i bit my nails off when you
asked me to come over
you might see i have freckles on my nose
i mean you brought me home because of the way i
looked in these clothes
can you look at me for a little longer with them
still on my body
please look at me and tell me one thing you don't
like

because maybe then i can believe that you see me
for me
and not for what comes after these clothes are on
the floor

_____

you are your father's daughter
that's what most people say to me
when they meet me for the first time

my mother says he's rotten
does that mean i'm rotten too?

_____

i wonder if i try to fix my lovers
because i couldn't fix my father

he's a broken man and i grew up watching
my mother try and piece him back together
and when she failed over and over again
i tried replacing the role

but no matter how hard i tried
i couldn't love him back together again
i think my father liked being broken
he liked replacing the role of my mother and i
he liked the idea of having different women
believe they could be the glue
that pieces him back together

there were times i thought he was fixed
the bandages covered his wounds
and he was almost good as new
almost.

until he'd slip up and break
just to prove that he was broken beyond repair
but the women he brought home were lucky.
my mother was lucky too.
they could leave the pieces for someone else to
pick up
i was nine picking up the pieces of my father
believing i would be the one to fix this

broken glass
but it kept cutting my fingers
and all i did was bleed.

after seven years i stopped trying to fix him
i gave up on him just like my mother
some people like to be broken
she used to tell me before she got out

i started gravitating towards broken people
i think i was ashamed i couldn't fix my father
so i tried fixing my lovers instead

i wish i had a softer obsession
one that didn't involve broken glass
i wanted to be loved delicately
but i stayed chasing razor blades instead

no matter how hard i tried fixing
the men in my life
i was always the one who ended up bleeding

so i guess i do try to fix my lovers
because i couldn't fix my father
i guess i just never thought
i would be the one who ended up broken

how come i put bandaids on everyone's wounds
but i'm the one still bleeding.

_____

i am the product of my parents
their dna is infiltrated throughout my body
my mother's heart
my father's eyes
my mother's sadness
my father's rage

their qualities rooted inside of me
even as i grow up
my feet are cemented to the ground
i can't escape
i can't escape this
i can't escape them

———

ever since i was little
my father joked that if we weren't careful
the floor of our house might fall through

i was a child
tiptoeing around the house
ever so carefully

i watched my mother do it too
but sometimes she misstepped
her face the color of snow

my father would turn to her
his body filling with rage so hot
he could have burned this house
to the ground

so i learned how to walk
on eggshells

———

you have such a nice house
my friends used to tell me
i'd respond with a *thank you*
and lightly brush it off

i mean they weren't wrong
i did grow up in a nice *house*

a nice front yard
a white picket fence
and a big red door.

but my house was never a home

you were not welcomed inside
by a mother dancing in the kitchen
cooking something on the stove

or a father with a plastered smile on his face
relaxing on the couch after work

i mean my father was a handyman
but he spent most of his time
making the outside of our house
perfect.

to ensure that no one would question
what went on inside of it.

———

my dad says he is hard on me
because he wants the best for me

he pushes me
because he wants to see my strength

he wants to make sure
that when he's not here
i won't still need him

 the little girl in me cries
"but i was only 9 and i needed you"

i still do

———

my father was not absent
he was always around
i think he loved me
he just couldn't show it

i got straight a's
and excelled in sports
i did everything.

i *lived* for my father

hoping that one day he would
tell me how much he loved me.

i met a guy at a party a couple weeks ago
he asked to take me home
i complied with no hesitation.

before we made it to his bedroom
my clothes were half off my body

maybe if i keep doing what he asks of me
he will want me back
i thought to myself
if i give him all the parts of me
he will tell me he loves me
but i don't know what more of myself

i have left to give.

please just tell me you love me

_____

people ask me what i wanna be when i grow up
and i think they are looking for
something tangible
like a teacher
or a psychologist
or an accountant.
but when i grow up i want to be kind
regardless of all of the bad things that have
happened to me in my life
i am not those bad things

i have the ability to wake up every day and be
one thing
i can choose to be kind

i still have a while left on this earth
and it can be pretty evil

i mean i was forced to grow up at a young age
seeing things no child should ever see
and hearing things no child should ever hear

some of my friends now tell me i'm their
comfort person
when they need to rant they come to me
or are looking for advice
or just someone to talk to
i think i needed someone kind growing up

no one knows how much violence it took me to be
this gentle
but that violence is what made me
me

so if i can wake up every day and have a choice to
be one thing
it will always be
to be kind

———

i think i'm the girl before the girlfriend
i wonder if i will always reside here
it's like being *the lid loosener*
i'll loosely open you up to the idea of
wanting love
but then you'll realize you don't want love
with me

i'm the test trial

you'll pick me up at night
and text me all day
but you'll screw the lid back on
and open it back up in a couple of weeks
with some new girl who is everything i am not

you use my heart to your advantage
breaking it to pieces over and over again
and then when you leave
and find someone else
you will take all the love i gave to you
and give it to her

i don't wanna be the step stool anymore
using me to get to the top

i don't wanna be the girl who teaches you how
to love
i want to be the girl who gets it

—————

2

fruit

spoiled fruit

i watched the blood drip between my legs when i
thought the tree had fully grown
i was ready for my cinderella moment
for someone to sweep me off my feet
look at me like i was the only girl in the world
see me through the darkness
and find the light inside of me

god i hope i'm ripe enough

_____

a tall man stood before me
with deep brown eyes
like the sweetest chocolate

he held out his hands in exchange for my heart
i stared at him with angst
like a beggar
pleading with him to take it
yet scared of the outcome of this
overwhelming gesture

i placed my heart in his hands gently
"please don't break it"

-eyes of a beggar

———

we laid on the grass
gazing at the stars
our bodies radiating warmth off of one another
i could hear his heart pound through his chest
i was at peace

i was the earth
and he was sun
my world constantly revolving around his

i wondered if he'd burn out
one day
when were older
wiser
smarter

what would happen then?
would the earth still spin?

- i hope it does

———

i was 15 when i met the boy on the beach
our eyes locked
and the world went quiet
we sat for hours
and whispered sweet nothings

the stillness of the world was disrupted by the
sound of my laugh
i forgot what it sounded like

i remember running home to my mother
my face radiating with sunshine
my heart warm
while the butterflies collided with one another
inside of my stomach
she looked at me with wide eyes
she looked at me with worry
almost like she had been here before
yet she smiled uncomfortably
and spoke to me through the voice of her
younger self
almost as if her first love was staring right back
at her
she told me she was happy for me
and offered me an orange

-my mother, the liar

_____

i vividly remember the first time a boy told me he
loved me
i stood about 4 feet out his front door walking
towards my car
the air was brisk
and i stood frozen as the words left his mouth
i looked at him puzzled
i couldn't wrap my head around the idea of
someone loving me for more than the fruit that
came between my legs

but will you love me in the winter
i replied
will you love me when my hair gets a little thinner
will you love me the next time the leaves fall from
the tree
will you love me when you're drunk and it's half
past three

i will love you with chapped lips
he replied
and extra fat around your hips
i will you love you on nights when you snore
and i'll still love you if you told me
you didnt wanna be here anymore

i will always love you

———

i was never scared of dying
i actually thought about it quite often
the thought of the world finally going quiet
a null
i was never scared of how life would carry on
without me here
maybe my dad would be confused
my sister would probably take my room (my
closets a little bigger)
and maybe my mom would stop buying oranges
from the grocery store
i was never scared of closing my eyes for one
last time
maybe the weight on my chest would go away
and feeling of suffocation would fade
i was never scared,
until you asked me to stay

———

i thought you had fully ripened
and i thought i had fully grown
as i ever so carefully
picked you off the tree

maybe my mother was right
when i peeled off your skin
you
were
rotten

i should've listened to my mother
when she spoke of spoiled fruit

———

you told me we were a bad idea
we would never work
we would be impossible
but i love challenges
and i told myself i would die before i lost this one
maybe it's the god complex in me
thinking i can fix everything that has been broken
love someone into loving me

i told you nothing was impossible
and i could win this game
i mean we've been playing it for years
and every time i got close to the finish line
you would draw a card that read
"go back 2 spaces"
i don't think you were playing by the rules
i think maybe you were just playing me

but rules are meant to be broken right
i mean that's what you told me
the night i found out about
her
you said it was never that deep
and you were just playing the game

i think you forgot to tell me that there was no
finish line
it was just an infinite cycle
me getting close to winning

and then you hitting me with a drawback

i mean that's not the only thing you hit me with
your words cut deep
but your fists cut deeper
i didn't even notice i was bleeding red
all i hoped
was that you would finally choose me
because after all
red was your favorite color

———

my mother told me he left me
because he was rotten
i told her he wasn't like dad

"maybe he wasn't bitter"
i said with a sour taste in my mouth
"maybe he was just 15"

‾‾‾‾‾

i thought the red that painted the insides of
my thighs
was symbolic
a sign that i was finally a woman
that the tree had fully grown

maybe i wasn't ripe enough

———

my mother held me
while i cried
she told me these were just growing pains

she said
"sometimes my darling, we have to grow away
from others,
so that we can grow into ourselves.
your first love will show you
what real love is not."

____

i gave myself to him with the skin peeled off
i let him see me for what was inside
i let him look at me raw

i let him memorize the lines that strung through
the palms of my hands
i let him count the number of veins that kept my
heart beating
and then allowed him to take out my heart with a
promise in exchange
a promise that he wouldn't be the one to break it

why did he only ever give me his skin

———

i thought your first love was supposed to be
what it looked like in movies
like five feet apart
or the notebook

i dreamt of that house
with blue shutters
and a room looking over the river

you dreamt of it too

but when you closed your eyes
and fell asleep

the life that you pictured
was a life without me in it

what does she have that i can't give you?

_____

to love you
was to hand you a gun
and have you aim it
at my heart
and pray
you never pull the trigger

———

save me an orange

my mother once told me to not perceive someone
from the outside
but to see them from within

sometimes we pick the brightest oranges
yet when we peel the skin away
their insides are rotten

should i have listened to my mother?

——

i looked in the mirror
my reflection stared back at me
focusing on the beat of my heart
thoughts consuming my brain
of the *what could've beens*
and the *what ifs*
the silence making me nauseous
i begin to feel like
the only girl in the world.
ironic.
isn't it?
i had once begged him
to make me feel like
the *only girl in the world.*

i'm not so sure
this is what i wanted after all.

———

i hate the fall
it smells like you again
and i can hear your voice
float through the wind

whispering those three little words

it's winter now
cold
and rainy
and you're not here

you promised to love me
through all of the seasons

maybe i was just not your weather.

———

what more did you want from me?
i gave you my heart
my soul
my body
i let you build a home inside of me

but you still went to the store
and bought a lighter

just to set me on fire

did you want to watch me burn?

———

you held me underwater
and every time i was beginning to drown
you'd briefly let me up for air
and then you would suffocate me all over again

the cycle that doesn't end

___

i was so afraid of finding someone
who was *nothing* like you

but now i'm afraid
of finding someone
who is *everything* like you

perspective

———

i remember the first time i found myself
being bitter
it was when i wondered for a little too long what
her perfume smells like

i pictured you holding her cheek and swiping her
blonde hair out of her eyes,
i see your pictures
(she hasn't taken them down)
do you, too,
look at them the way i do?
did you rub the tip of your nose to hers
as you did to mine?
i'm sure you promised her forever

is that the same forever you promised me?

———

i remember the night you came home late
i knew what you had done
you didn't have to say anything
your eyes told me all i needed to know

i didn't ask who she was
i simply asked
"how was your night?"

"fine. how was yours?"

now i couldn't accuse you of being a liar

but god you were a fucking coward.

to be the liar, or be the coward

———

i woke up to a text from you today
you asked if we could meet up to "talk"
i should've known better
because "talking" doesn't really mean "talking"

talking means your hand on my thigh
while you whisper in my ear
how sorry you are
and suddenly your fingers
are scraping my insides

and i want you to stop
but i don't tell you to
i just want to pretend a little while longer
i want to believe for a second
that i really am what you want
crave me for a little longer

please, just five more minutes

_____

i started to justify all of my scars
because i loved the person
who was holding the knife

did you kill me
or did i kill myself?

———

"stop looking at me like that"

"like what?" he replied

"like i am someone you could actually love."

———

i hate you

i hate that i pick up my phone
in hopes of you texting me
i hate that i can't delete the pictures of us
and i hate the knot you left
sitting in my stomach
i hate that you stole the best parts of me

can you steal the pain too?

———

i don't know who i hate more

you
or
myself

i hate you for coming back
every time you feel lonely

but i hate myself
for letting you back in
every time you beg for my love

i think i hate myself more

_____

i went on my first date today
well not really my first

the first date since you left me

we sat in his car
and laughed

he abruptly reached in front of my knees
for something in his glove compartment

i flinched.

he looked at me frozen

the way you look at a broken glass
after knocking it to the ground
knowing it can't be fixed.

———

"someone will love me in more ways than you
ever did"

i screamed as tears ran down my face

he replied back to me

with zero sign of life
behind his eyes

"no one wants bruised fruit."
_____

i always wondered what my father saw in you
why he cared for you like a son
why he never questioned my tears
or the bruises on my body
why *he still asked about you* after you left me

i think my father found comfort
in seeing himself in you

i guess the apple doesn't fall far from the tree

———

save me an orange

my father was the first person
to take the life out of me

and i promise
you will be the last

_____

maybe you were right to call me "insane"
the definition of "insane" is
doing the same thing
over and over again
yet expecting a different result.

i let you come back
over and over again

believing you will come back
as the version i have of you
in my head

but you never do
and i continue to leave a spare key
under the mat of my front door

i think it's time to throw away the spare

———

save me an orange

my mother may have mentioned spoiled fruit
but she forgot to tell me
when you put rotten fruit
next to good fruit
the good fruit becomes spoiled too

you turned me rotten

_____

oranges

my friend asked me to write a poem about the
right person wrong time
but truthfully i don't think the right person comes
at the wrong time
i think they are just the wrong person
because if it was meant to be it simply would just
be

i think we tell ourselves this as a way to cope
it's better to believe they were the right person
than admit they aren't mature enough to love you
the right person doesn't leave because of
the distance
he doesn't leave because he wants to grow
he doesn't leave because you deserve better

the right person will see you deserve better and
choose to be better

so i guess i can't
i can't write a poem about the right person who
comes at the wrong time
because they do not exist
but i guess i can write a poem about the
wrong person

the wrong person will teach you to love yourself
every day
the wrong person will show you that there is a life
after them

one filled with joy, laughter, tears, and even pain
the wrong person will remind you to choose
yourself every day
the wrong person helps you find yourself
and they will lead you to the right person
but this time
the right time.

———

and when he tells you he is sorry,
look at him politely and tell him about the river.
the river in which he built, out of tears
that he so viciously grasped from your eyes.
the ones that fell from your cheek
after asking yourself that million dollar question,
for the 22nd night in a row.
"why am i not good enough?
when he tells you he is sorry,
stare deeply into his brown eyes
and remind him of the pieces of glass
that are still left on the floor.
the pieces you refused to pick up
after he gauged a broken piece into your heart
as he watched the blood drip to the floor.
the blood that stains the ground,
the sheets, the walls.
tell him that you put the glass back together
but the blood won't come out.

the blood is what lingers,
on the ground, the sheets, the walls.
tell him it lingers when you drive past that
restaurant
you used to go to.
and tell him it lingers
when that song comes on the radio.
and tell him that, even after you used
the whole bottle of bleach,

it lingers in every place that he touched.
and every time you look in the mirror
you see the blood that is traced
over all of the places that were just for him.
tell him that you stopped looking in the mirror.
tell him that you stopped listening to the radio.
tell him that you take a new way home,
just so you don't pass that restaurant.
and when he tells you he is sorry
i hope you finally have the strength back
of the woman you built back up from the ground
to tell him he cannot be sorry,
because his hands are what still bleed
red.

———

there's a quote that says
"people don't stop playing
because they grew up,
people grow up
because they stopped playing."

never stop playing.
go outside
call your best friend on her home phone
like you used to do when you were kids
buy lemons and make lemonade
or better yet
pick oranges from a tree
and make orange juice

you are every age you have ever been.
you were not put on this earth
to sit here
and rot
you are not the spoiled fruit
he made you think you were

you were put on this earth to live
it's not too late
to start now

_____

i hope one day you find me in a grocery store
i'll have new tattoos
but my perfume will stay the same
our eyes will lock
while i stand beside an aisle of fruit
your heart sinks to the ground
and i'll lose my voice
all over again

we will laugh about how long it's been
and you will apologize
for your immaturities

i'll wish you well
and before you're on your way
i'll remind you to not feel guilty
because after all
we were only 15.

——

"i'll never be the same again."
i said to myself
as i sobbed on my cold bathroom floor
after leaving your house for the last time

i left pieces of my heart on your bedroom floor
that night
how could my heart still be aching
when there was no heart left in me anymore

i was so afraid of the person i would be
without you
that i never thought about
the person i could be without you

i never thought this far
i never thought of a life after you
for all the time we spent together
i only pictured a life with you in it

but now i know
because there was a life after you
and it was beautiful
and sweet
and sometimes scary

but i don't have to wear rose colored glasses
to see life in color anymore

i don't have to wait up hoping you will call
i don't have to pretend to be sleeping to see the
girls' names on your phone
i don't have to do any of the things i never wanted
to do in the first place

i don't have to be that girl anymore
and i can confidently say
"i'll never be the same again."

———

the younger version of you
that still lives inside of you

would be so proud
of the version of yourself
that stands in front of
the mirror today

a message from your younger self

_____

some of my friends don't talk about
their relationships
in fear of judgment
or ridicule
afraid i'll look at them and laugh
accuse them of being weak
not leaving a relationship
that no longer serves them

but i've walked this path before
not very long ago
i know what it's like to stand before a man
and ask him
"how small do you want me"
i know what it's like to be robbed
of your heart
your voice
and the fruit that comes between your legs

and i know what it's like to stay
in the comfort of their navy blue sheets
or the comfort of their voice
or the comfort of the hands that hold you
so tight
maybe sometimes a little too tight
it's like you're suffocating

and you can't breathe

i know what it's like to want out
but when you try and speak
no words leave your mouth
because he robbed you of your voice
yet he still left you with enough
so that you can still ask him
"how small do you want me"

now i can't tell you it won't be scary
but i can tell you life after him has been sweet
stop making yourself small
just so you're easier for him to swallow
let. him. choke.

_____

it's been 2 years now
you would assume that after this long of
separation from a person
you would soon forget
but this isn't a love poem
no.
you would think after this long i would have
found someone new
someone smart
and brave
someone that knows how to make me laugh
and knows all my favorite foods.
but no.
this isn't a love poem
i promise i'm over you
i'm over you until i walk past some random kid in
the library who smells just like you
i'm over you until they play our favorite song on
the speaker
i'm over you until someone says that silly
little saying
the one only you and i had known about.
but no.
this isn't a love poem.
i promise i'm over you
i'm over you until it's 2am

and i see your name on my phone
right after a night out

but i don't dare to watch your stories
i don't want to know anything about you
i don't want to know who you are now
or what your favorite scent is now
and no.
i don't want to know your favorite tv shows
or what your new favorite song is
i don't want to know because this isn't a
love poem
i tell myself i'm over you
until it's the 5th of every month
when i look in the mirror
and see glimpses of you in the reflection
our eyes become one
and it's a staring contest
me against you
but i win every time
no this isn't a love poem
because after looking in the mirror for so long
i can see what i have made of myself
it's been 2 years since you have touched me
and i like it this way
i have made it so far with your absence
i have finally had the ability to love someone
other than you
and that person is me
no this isn't a love poem
because you were never there to pick me up when
i cried

you weren't there when i told my mom i didn't
wanna be here anymore
you weren't there when i got accepted into my
dream school
and you weren't there to tell me everything was
going to be okay
i was.
i was there for myself every time
every time you got my hopes up
every time you let me down
i picked myself up every time
and i thrived
i thrived every single time
all in the absence of you
so maybe i lied
maybe this is a love poem
not one to you
but to myself
so thank you
thank you for showing me that i never needed
someone to make me feel special
or loved
or unique
or smart
thank you for reminding me that i will always be
the love of my own life.

_____

i failed my math test today
it was cold and rainy
which didn't help
when i was 14 i didn't think this
would've mattered
but the world didn't end when i was 16

i've loved a lot of people
most of them never deserved my energy
i've been used
replaced
forgotten
and reused again
all because
the world didn't end
when i was 16

me and my dad got in a fight today
we argued over spilt milk
we screamed in the kitchen
his words like knives
i wanted to bleed out
all because the world didn't end
when i was 16

when i turned 16
the world kept spinning
so i went out on most fridays
and danced with my friends

save me an orange

i mean if the world was still spinning
i couldn't just stand on it
i sat at the kitchen table
with a bottle of wine
and my childhood friends
we laughed so hard
we could no longer speak
all because
the world didn't end
when i was 16

i got up this morning
and went to the beach
the sun crept up over the horizon
and i felt warm inside
while the wind whistled through the sky
and the breeze left chills down my spine
i smiled and thought
"oh what a beautiful life"
all because the world didn't end when i was 16

even when you think there's nothing left
life gives us oranges
so go share one with your best friend
maybe she thought the world would end
when she was 16 too

———

an old friend stopped by my house the other day
and before she left she looked at me and asked
"but what if it doesn't get better?"

and i think that's where she has it all wrong
not every day is going to be good
not every day is going to be easy
there will be days when all you do is lay in
your bed
there will be days where you skip breakfast
lunch
or dinner
there will be days where you pity yourself
and on some days you will make a mistake or two

but it's a good thing you have tomorrow
and if you don't get it right tomorrow
you still have the day after that

your life will be what you make of it
so if today was not your best day
try again tomorrow.

and before my friend walked out my front door
i looked at her and laughed
"but what if it does get better?'

_____

not everyone who leaves
is going to come back
you won't go back
to every place you have traveled to
you can't go back in time
the past is in the past
and it won't come back

but if i have learned one thing
it is that the only thing
that can always come back
is love
love leaves
but always returns
sometimes in the form of a person
or a song
maybe a book
or even a hobby

love always comes back

_____

i hate how we normalize ex lovers coming back
when you go through a breakup
and your friends tell you not to worry
because "they always come back"
and it's funny because they aren't wrong

it's like when you desperately try and move on
for months
and when you finally move on
they move back in
and the cycle constantly repeats

it is comforting for a little while
until it's not, really
you get to a point where you wanna ask them
not to

but you don't because you find comfort in the fact
that maybe just maybe they could love you how
they used to
and you realize you finally were taking a
step forward
for one simple message to take you a
leap backwards

and now you're here and the cycle repeats again.
and i can tell you it really isn't that they care
when they send you a "hey how are you" message

it's not because they are actually concerned about
how you are
ex's come back when they feel that leash they had
you on
is starting to get a little too long
and that rope is starting to thin out
you're moving too far away from them
and they can't reel you back in

so you wake up to a message from them
after months of no contact
and when you respond
they feel a sense of relief

the truth is exes don't come back because they are
interested
they come back because they want to make sure
you're still here

so let's stop playing the role
of the puppy dog on the leash
who runs home to their owner when they hear the
sound of their name

let's normalize cutting the rope
let it thin out
and run

run so far and never look back
nothing good comes from running back to
someone who set the house on fire with you in it
so save yourself
and let him burn.

———

your sister never asked you to love her
did she?
your best friend never called you at 3am
begging for you to love her
the way she loves you
did she?
you curse at your mother
yet before you leave the house
you still remember to tell her you love her

none of these people asked you to love them
none of these people pleaded and begged
for your love

yet you still love them.

you give your dog food from the dinner table
when no one's looking
because you love your dog

and when you come home from a long day
your dog greets you at the door
with kisses and excitement

but your dog doesn't have to tell you
he loves you in order for you to know that
does he?

sometimes we think we are unloveable
but we are really just asking the wrong people to
love us

you should never ask someone to love you
beg for them to find you in the darkness and show
you the light

you will never have to beg the right person to
love you
if you have to beg
then you are begging the wrong person

your mother didn't look at the hair on your arm
and decide one day she wasn't gonna love
you anymore.

your best friend watched you eat a second and
third slice of pizza and i bet she still loves
you too.

you are not unlovable because you didn't have
time to straighten your hair
you are not unlovable because you ordered a coke
instead of diet
you are not unloveable if all you did today
was exist
for every one person who could not love
you correctly

i bet you could name five people who can
and even if you can't

your dog will still be waiting behind the door
to love you when you come home.

———

one day you will realize
you don't have to love someone
into loving you.
you don't have to fix everything
that has been broken

some broken things can't be fixed
and some broken people
don't want to be.

don't think less of yourself
because they can't be more for themselves

-----

i'm over you
and this time i mean it
i can watch your friends stories
see pictures of your face
and feel nothing towards you
the gravitational pull between us
is gone

and now when i see a flashback of us
you're not the one i'm looking at
it's me
i stare at my smile
my eyes
so captivated by love

a couple of years ago i'd stare at the pictures of us
together
and beg for you back
but now i stare at the pictures of myself with you
in them
and beg for myself back

i may have been unhealthily in love
addicted to you like a drug
that i didn't read the side effects of
maybe i should've read the fine print
ive finally been able to cut myself off
and i'm going through withdrawals
not withdrawing from you
but from the feeling of love

i miss my laugh and my smile
and the times when i saw the world in color

they say drugs come with side effects
but i didn't expect this one
you took the life out of me
and i'm begging for it back

maybe this year
i'll find love again
but this time i'll know better
and i'll read the fine print

———

my friend from college asked me
"what's your biggest regret?"

and a couple years ago
i would've had a list

of people i've met
and situations
i put myself in.

but when people ask me now
"what's your biggest regret?"

i laugh.
if i regret meeting certain people
and i regret certain paths
that life has taken me

would i be as strong as i am now?
would i be the person i am today?
would i even be me at all?

the ghost of the woman i never was

_____

so when you find yourself
sitting on the bathroom floor
in silence because
the boy you met at 16
found a new lover
and the girl you grew up with
down the street from you
stops answering your calls
and your father's words
still cut between your veins
or because your shampoo
and conditioner
ran out at the same time.

don't submit to your sadness
and drown beneath your tears

get up.
go to the store.
and buy some more.

and while you are there…

stop by the fruit section
and pick up an orange for yourself

but before you head to the register
grab a second piece of fruit.

save me an orange too.

_____

acknowledgements

thank you to all the people who didn't let their world end at sixteen. this book would have never been possible without your love and support. you have given me the ability to have a voice, and speak for the people who haven't found theirs yet and i could not be more grateful.

i cannot thank my friends enough for encouraging me throughout this journey, reading my rough drafts, and giving me advice. this book would not have come to life without you. and lastly, to sage cunningham thank you for believing in me and for being the first person who made me believe in myself. i would have never had the opportunity to share my art with the world if i never met you. thank you.

for the people who want to continue listening to random thoughts i read, you can find me on all my social media platforms…. @hayleygracepoetry

Printed in Great Britain
by Amazon

45249479R00067